PATTERNS OF CHILDHOOD

Samplers from Glasgow Museums

PATTERNS OF CHILDHOOD

Samplers from Glasgow Museums

Rebecca Quinton

The Herbert Press
an imprint of A&C Black

in association with Glasgow City Council (Museums)

First published in 2005 by The Herbert Press
an imprint of A&C Black Publishers
37 Soho Square
London W1D 3QZ
www.acblack.com

in association with Glasgow City Council (Museums)

ISBN-10: 0 7136 7476 8
ISBN-13: 978 0 7136 7476 7

Text by Rebecca Quinton, Curator, Costume and Textiles,
Glasgow Museums.
Edited by Vivien Hamilton and Susan Pacitti
Designed by Proof Books
Photographs, unless otherwise indicated, are from Glasgow City Council (Museums)
Photo Library and Photography Department.

The publishers gratefully acknowledge the following for permission to
reproduce illustrations:

'Dancing class in the schoolroom at New Lanark', reproduced by kind
permission of the New Lanark Conservation Trust, www.newlanark.org

Photograph of Ackworth School reproduced by kind permission of
Ackworth School.

'Elizabeth Fry reading to the prisoners at Newgate, 1816', an engraving by
T Oldham Barlow after an oil painting by Jerry Barrett (1824–1906), reproduced
by kind permission of the Library of the Religious Society of Friends,
www.quaker.org.uk

www.glasgowmuseums.com

This publication was produced to accompany the exhibition
Patterns of Childhood: Samplers 1640-1900, Scotland Street School Museum, Glasgow,
30 April – 26 September 2005.

Contents

Introduction

What is a sampler?

The term sampler comes from the French *essamplaire*, meaning example. It is used to refer to a piece of material embroidered with a variety of different stitches and patterns – part practice and part reference. For many centuries needlework was a fundamental part of a young girl's education, and samplers played a key role in the teaching of those skills.

The earliest surviving dated sampler in Britain was made in 1598 by Jane Bostocke, and is now in the Victoria & Albert Museum, London. Early samplers can be divided generally into two types – the spot motif sampler and the band sampler. Spot motif samplers are so called because of the variety of individual motifs sewn randomly across the fabric; band samplers are named after their long, narrow shape, cut from the end width of a roll of linen. Both were popular during the seventeenth and early eighteenth centuries when samplers were made as reference tools for patterns to be sewn onto household linen. One of the most popular sources for the designs of this period was John Taylor's *The Needles Excellency: A New Booke wherin are divers Admirable Workes wrought with the Needle*, published in 1631.

Many schools were founded during the eighteenth century, and making samplers became an integral part of a girl's education. However, technical ability appears to have diminished in later years, as it became less important for pupils to master a large range of complicated stitches. Samplers were no longer seen as the first stage towards becoming an accomplished needlewoman. Instead they were a means of learning the basic sewing and pattern cutting skills required for professional employment as a maid, teacher or seamstress. New elements, such as geography, mathematics and morality were introduced. By 1900 most samplers no longer featured decorative embroidery, but demonstrated plain sewing techniques, including hemming and basic dressmaking.

Samplers in Glasgow Museums' collections

Glasgow Museums is fortunate to have two important groups of samplers, divided between the Burrell Collection and the costume and textiles collection. By uniting the two collections in this publication we can trace the development of samplers over a period of 300 years, from the early seventeenth century to the early twentieth century.

Sir William Burrell (1861–1958), a wealthy shipping magnate, was an avid collector of art. He amassed a large collection of objects from all over the world, which he gifted to the city of Glasgow in 1944. His collection of British embroidery is of the finest quality and includes 26 samplers, most of which date from the seventeenth century. He bought one of his first samplers in 1916, for £39.18.0. He continued to buy samplers over the next 30 years from top London dealers and larger department stores, such as Debenham and Freebody, paying about £40 for each. Several were used to furnish his home, Hutton Castle, in the Scottish Borders. Others he lent to museums and exhibitions.

The costume and textiles collection currently includes around 200 samplers, most of which date from the eighteenth and nineteenth centuries. The earliest acquisition, a sampler made by Jane Chapman in 1827, was purchased in 1896; the most recent, made by Mary Thomson in 1903, was collected in 2003. The majority of the samplers have been donated to Glasgow Museums, often by the descendants of the maker. Purchases are relatively rare, exceptions being particularly interesting or unusual samplers that come up at auction.

Most of the samplers in both collections were acquired because of their inherent charm or the skill of the needlework. Today's practice of placing museum objects within their social context has highlighted how little is known about many of these samplers, especially about the lives of their makers. Ongoing research over the last 20 years by museum staff and volunteers has answered some questions, but in turn has identified further areas of enquiry. Many Scottish samplers include the names or initials of the maker's family, and are increasingly being used as a source for tracing family trees. As official records, such as the 10-yearly National Census, are made more accessible it is hoped that in the future we will find out further details about the elusive makers of these beautiful samplers.

Rebecca Quinton
Curator, Costume and Textiles
Glasgow Museums

1. Sampler made in England, circa 1625–1630

52 cm (20 1/2 in.) x 33.6 cm (13 1/4 in.)

Samplers such as this, with its range of randomly scattered individual and often unlinked motifs, are known as 'spot motif' samplers. This is one of the earliest surviving forms of sampler that still survives and was popular during the first half of the seventeenth century. The motifs worked on this example are particularly diverse. At the top are geometric designs, including in the far left a small section of Florentine work – also known as Bargello or flame stitch – with its rows of coloured zigzag lines.

On the right, the three small naturalistic flowers shown complete with their stalks are similar to the slips popular during the late sixteenth and early seventeenth centuries. Named after gardeners' cuttings, or slips, these floral motifs embroidered in tent or cross stitch were individually cut out and applied to a wide range of domestic furnishings, such as bed and wall hangings, cushions and curtains. They were copied from drawings of flora and fauna printed in contemporary herbals and pattern books, such as John Gerard's *Herbal or General History of Plants*, published in 1597.

Squeezed in at the bottom of the sampler are two delicately drawn royal ciphers, or monograms. The first cipher, with initials 'CR' for *Carolus Rex* (King Charles), has a crown and the Tudor red and white petal rose with traditional Royalist lion and unicorn supporters (animals holding up a coat of arms) on either side. The second has the initials 'ER', possibly for *Elizabeth Regina* (Queen Elizabeth), with foliage around the rose in place of the supporters.

This sampler dates from between 1625 and 1630, and is one of the earliest held in the Burrell Collection. It has been worked on unbleached plain, or tabby, weave linen embroidered in vibrant polychrome silk threads enhanced with additional silver thread. The silver thread, now blackened by time, would have sparkled when it caught the light.

2. Sampler made in England, circa 1630–1650

52.7 cm (20 3/4 in.) x 26 cm (10 1/4 in.)

An accomplished embroiderer made this colourful and rather busy spot motif sampler, combining basic stitches with raised and padded work.

Amongst the simpler floral motifs, shown with the flower heads standing proud on their stalks, are roses and carnations or pinks. More flamboyant are the flowers worked with three-dimensional petals, each outlined with silver gilt thread and set within diamond-shaped (or lozenge-shaped as they were known then) beds bordered with smaller flowers. This is reminiscent of the formal knot gardens and parterres found in the most fashionable gardens of the period.

Scattered in between, as if to assist with the pollination of the flowers, are butterflies, insects and birds. At the bottom right corner lurks a rather incongruous fish gasping for breath!

3. White work sampler made by Judith Fisher, England, circa 1640

25.4 cm (10 in.) x 22.8 cm (9 in.)

Girls who had mastered more complex stitches went on to make white work samplers such as this charming example. White work requires not only advanced needlework skills, but also extremely good eyesight to work with the fine white threads against a white background. This is generally regarded as one of the most difficult forms of needlework, with the most admired being the exquisitely embroidered Ayrshire white work infants' gowns of the mid-nineteenth century.

This white work sampler combines bands embroidered in white silk with rows of cut and drawn work, where threads within the weave of the linen are cut, drawn out and worked into intricate patterns. The bottom two bands have rows of squares painstakingly cut out of the linen, leaving a grid of only a few threads as the basis of the needlework. The last row is unfinished and shows the various stages of development. Still attached is the backing paper used to support the grid while it was worked, inscribed with the maker's name, 'Judith Ffisher' (sic). The majority of these white work samplers are anonymous, and it is ironic that by leaving her piece unfinished Judith created a lasting name for herself.

4. Sampler made in England, mid-17th century

43.1 cm (17 in.) x 58.4 cm (23 in.)

This fascinating sampler has a romantic association with Mary of Modena, the second wife of James, Duke of York (later James VII of Scotland and II of England). It was previously in the collection of the Countess of Ranfurly, where it was described as the sampler of Mary Este, d'Este being Mary's maiden name. However, it remains a mystery as to whether the sampler was actually made by Mary, or whether it was just one of her many household goods. After her husband was deposed during the Glorious Revolution of 1688, Mary was forced to flee to France, leaving most of her belongings behind.

The sampler is neatly embroidered on linen with colourful silk threads in a variety of spot motifs. Some of these are unfinished, and interestingly show the original line drawings beneath. The motifs on the left are similar to those found on slips (see sampler 1), with a variety of flowering stems including a poppy, carnation and rose, interspersed with busy insects and birds. The caterpillars and butterflies would have been interpreted as Royalist symbols at that time – the caterpillar representing Charles I, and the butterfly the restoration of Charles II.

Standing amongst these delightful motifs is the incomplete figure of a woman, possibly a representation of Flora or Spring. She is wearing the short-waisted dress with large puffed and slashed sleeves and small square standing collar, or ruff, that was fashionable during the 1630s. At her feet sits her obedient companion, wagging his tail.

In complete contrast, the right half of the sampler is worked with a series of stylized motifs and various abstract geometric and diaper patterns in cross, eyelet and rococo stitch. It is possible that someone else may have embroidered this section at a later date.

5. Sampler made in England, mid-17th century

94.6 cm (37 1/4 in.) x 17.8 cm (7 in.)

The long, narrow shape of this sampler is typical of many made during the seventeenth century, and is called a 'band sampler'. The linen has been cut horizontally from the end of a long length of material, leaving the selvage visible at both ends. It was then embroidered with rows of floral and geometric border patterns in brightly coloured silk threads.

After completing her sampler, a young girl would progress to making small needlework panels, often illustrating biblical or classical scenes. Some of these she may have sent to a local cabinetmaker to be made up into an embroidered box or casket, similar to that shown here. Inside would be stored sewing equipment, including the band sampler carefully rolled up, and treasured keepsakes, sometimes hidden in secret compartments.

Needlework casket, late 17th century, Burrell Collection.

6. Sampler made in England, mid-17th century

92.7 cm (36 1/2 in.) x 18.4 cm (7 1/4 in.)

This is a perfect example of the sampler as a reference tool. The wide variety of patterns worked here would have offered plenty of inspiration to the amateur needleworker for decorative borders on her family's bed and table linen. An example of this use can be seen on the pillowcase border shown below.

Particularly eye-catching are the band with the two intriguing figures known as 'boxers', due to their pose (also found on samplers 7, 8 and 18), and the delicate monochrome designs worked mainly in double-running and stem stitch.

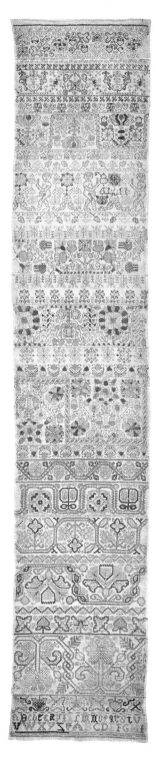

7. Sampler made in England, mid-17th century

90.1 cm (35 1/2 in.) x 17.8 cm (7 in.)

A girl would be spoilt for choice when selecting which border design to use on her pillowcases from those worked on this band sampler. Near the top the popular boxer pattern (see samplers 6, 8 and 18) with its posturing male figures can be seen.

Further down there are variations on a floral border, with meandering, and in some cases, twisted stems. The version at the bottom, with its large poppies, must have been from a well-known source, as it appears on several other seventeenth-century samplers in the Burrell Collection (see samplers 13, 15 and 18). Many of these border patterns disappeared from use during the eighteenth century as wider samplers with central panels became fashionable. However, this particular design with the stylized intertwining stems continued to be used on many Scottish samplers well into the nineteenth century (see samplers 20, 23, 33, 39 and 41).

8. Sampler made in England, mid-17th century

104.1 cm (41 in.) x 20.3 cm (8 in.)

The two quizzical figures in black with wide-brimmed hats are a variation of the boxers found on several samplers of the period (see samplers 6, 7 and 18). Their name derives from their boxer-like stance with legs astride and forearms lifted, although a real pugilist might find such a posture of little practical use in a contest!

This is a misnomer, however, and it is more likely that this popular motif derives from the classical Greek *erotes*, a pair of lovers exchanging tokens such as flowers or plants. Indeed, plants appear to be what the figures are presenting to each other on this sampler.

Over the centuries the drawing of the amorous pair has gradually changed. This is particularly apparent on seventeenth-century English samplers, where it is not always clear what the male figure is doing and the poor female figure has metamorphosed into a strangely shaped bush or shrub. In this sampler, the outline of the female's head, body and extended arm can still just be seen. Originally the figures were depicted naked, but increasingly they wear doublets and breeches or, as in this instance, some form of body-hugging all-in-one outfit.

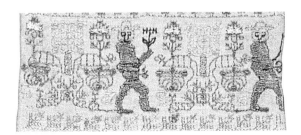

9. White work sampler made in England, mid-17th century

74.9 cm (29 1/2 in.) x 14 cm (5 1/2 in.)

During the seventeenth century beautiful high-quality lace was fashionable both for clothing and for decorating bed and table linen. The wealthier members of society were able to afford expensive needle lace imported from Holland and Italy, while aspiring middle-class ladies with less disposable income copied the lacelike patterns found on white work samplers.

The unfinished nature of this sampler gives its finely worked rows a delicate and fragile appearance. Far from being discarded for its incompleteness, it is prized by today's needleworker, who relishes the opportunity of seeing the different stages in the working of these wonderful white work samplers. The rows at the top clearly show how certain threads within the weave of the linen have been cut and removed to form the foundation of the design.

10. Sampler made by A Austen, Great Britain, 1663

74.2 cm (29 1/4 in.) x 17.1 cm (6 3/4 in.)

This is the earliest dated sampler in the collection with an alphabet worked on it, a common characteristic of later samplers. Interestingly, both alphabets on this sampler, as on several other seventeenth- and eighteenth-century samplers, omit the letters 'J' and 'U'.

During the seventeenth century the letters 'J' and 'I' were used interchangeably, and as a result do not appear separately in many alphabets until the nineteenth century. The absence of the written letter 'U' dates back to ancient Rome, when stonemasons found the letter hard to carve and used 'V' instead. This tradition was continued by the monks and did not change until printers in the eighteenth century began to standardize characters. So, as with the interchangeable 'I' and 'J', either a 'U' or 'V' is used on samplers until the nineteenth century, when increasingly all 26 letters of the alphabet are used. This was the result of the increased spread of the printed word and the introduction of more uniform teaching in schools.

11. Sampler made by Frances Cheyney, England, 1663

60.9 cm (24 in.) x 18.4 cm (7 1/4 in.)

Although this sampler with its long narrow form with border patterns continues in the tradition of seventeenth-century band samplers, the inclusion of a central tableau, or scene, anticipates the change towards the shorter, broader samplers of the eighteenth century.

At first glance, the pastoral scene seems a charming depiction of rural pursuits. However, the prominence of the oak tree laden with acorns and the inclusion of the acorns in one of the borders above suggest an underlying symbolism. The oak tree is traditionally associated with Charles II. During the Civil War, after the Battle of Worcester, Charles spent a night hiding in a large oak tree at Boscobel House in Shropshire. When he was restored to the throne in 1660, he established the Order of the Royal Oak to show his gratitude to those who had helped him.

The acorn is also a symbol of rebirth, and became associated with the return of the monarchy. The inclusion of these motifs may well reflect the general joy resulting from the restoration of the monarchy. An almost identical scene of a male figure beside an oak tree but with a castle in the background appears in a sampler in the Fitzwilliam Museum in Cambridge.

12. White work sampler made by Frances Cheyney, England, 1664

64.7 cm (25 1/2 in.) x 20.3 cm (8 in.)

The identities of the figures in this sampler are uncertain. Many of the mid-seventeenth-century needlework panels depict biblical scenes, particularly those with strong female characters such as Esther, Susanna or Judith. This sampler is thought to show the story of Judith.

In the apocryphal Book of Judith (Chapter 13), Judith's native town of Bethulia was laid siege by the invading Assyrian army under the command of Holofernes. In order to save the town and her people, Judith cut Holofernes' head off while he was asleep. She then gave the decapitated head to her maid, who smuggled it out of the camp in a bag of meat. Women had to defend their family, political beliefs, and often their households and property during the instability of the Civil Wars, and Judith was lauded as a role model. Alternatively, instead of showing Judith, her maid and the head of Holofernes, the figures may just be a depiction of a woman with her child and a long-whiskered cat!

Made a year later than Frances' embroidered sampler (see sampler 11), this white work sampler shows her continuing accomplishment as a needleworker. Its eight rows of cut and drawn threadwork include additional areas of delicate needlepoint filling, weaving and some raised and padded work. The only use of colour is the light pink silk thread used to embroider the cheeks and mouths of the two female figures.

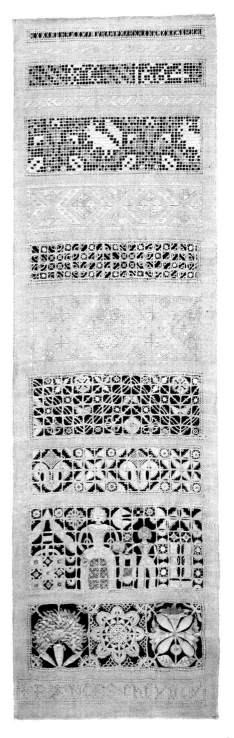

13. Sampler made by Elizabeth Fares, England, 1664

52 cm (20 1/2 in.) x 22.8 cm (9 in.)

Dominating the centre of this colourful sampler is a large symmetrical representation of the flower columbine. The flower's common name derives from the Latin word *columba*, meaning dove, as its flowers are said to resemble a ring of five doves. It is sometimes seen as another symbol for the Holy Spirit.

The flower's Latin name, *aquilegia*, is either a derivation of *aquila*, meaning eagle, or *aquilegus*, meaning water container, reflecting the up-turned bucket-like petals. According to Christian tradition the flower is associated with the Virgin Mary, and said to have sprung up where her feet trod as she walked to meet Elizabeth, the mother of John the Baptist. However, by the seventeenth century the flower had become a symbol of adultery, as its spur-like petals were reminiscent of cuckold's horns. In Shakespeare's *Hamlet*, columbine is one of the flowers Ophelia gives to King Claudius as a sign of his infidelity.

At the top, embroidered rather cryptically upside down, are the alphabet and the inscription 'ELEZZEBETH FAREZ ROYGHT THIS SAMPLER Ended IN THE 4 DAY OF APRIL 1664'. This suggests that some of these band samplers may have been worked from both ends of their length – perhaps for reasons of economy, or ease of stitching.

23

14. Sampler made by Jane Turner, England, 1668

66 cm (26 in.) x 16.5 cm (6 1/2 in.)

The central and rather dominant figure of a woman seen on this sampler may be a depiction of Flora (see sampler 4), with her large crown of flowers and holding blossom in her hand. She is fashionably dressed in an open gown with a falling collar, neatly worked in detached buttonhole stitch. Together with the padded face this may suggest that the sampler was made as practice for a later embroidered panel featuring raised and padded work, such as the one shown below.

Jane Turner appears to have been an accomplished needleworker, as she combines a wide variety of stitches in this sampler. The finely drawn borders at the top are embroidered in running, stem, trellis and Montenegrin stitches amongst others. The design is similar to another sampler made by Mary Lawley, dated 1668, now in a private collection. Perhaps both girls attended the same school.

Needlework panel depicting Abraham casting out Hagar and Ishmael, mid-17th century, Burrell Collection.

15. Sampler made by CP and Elizabeth Priest, England, 1674 and 1676

75.5 cm (29 3/4 in.) x 24.7 cm (9 3/4 in.)

This intriguing sampler, with its contrasting styles at top and bottom, appears to have been made by two sisters. The lower half is embroidered with traditional rows of border patterns, including various versions of the poppy with twisted stems, and is signed upside down in the bottom right corner 'CP 74'. The sampler was completed two years later, making economical use of the leftover linen, and is inscribed 'ELIZABETH PRIEST IS MY NAME AND WITH MY NEDLE 76' at the top.

Elizabeth's half of the sampler is rather striking, with its use of large figural motifs including a stag within a bower hiding from a huntsman and his hounds. Above, filling the width of the band, is a large depiction of a Pelican in Piety – a term from heraldry and symbolic art – with the female bird shown pecking at her breast to draw blood to feed her young chicks in the nest below. This is thought to derive from early ornithological confusion over the pelican's habit of feeding its young half-digested food from the pouch below its bill. This belief was repeated in most medieval bestiaries (books of beasts). For centuries the Pelican in Piety was a symbol of self-sacrifice, specifically of Christ's death. One of the first written references appears in the hymn 'Adoro Te Devote' by Thomas Aquinas – 'Pie Pellicane, Jesu Domine, Me immundum munda Tuo sanguine' (O Loving Pelican, O Jesu Lord, Unclean am I but cleanse me in Thy blood).

A similar depiction of the Pelican in Piety appears on a sampler by Jane Bostocke, dated 1598, now in the Victoria & Albert Museum, and on several seventeenth-century Germanic samplers.

16. Sampler made in England, circa 1650–1700

58.4 cm (23 in.) x 17.8 cm (7 in.)

One of the best known and most copied pattern books available to well-to-do amateur needleworkers in the seventeenth century was *The Needles Excellency: A New Booke wherin are divers Admirable Workes wrought with the Needle* by John Taylor, published in 1631. The much-quoted poem 'The Praise of the Needle' prefaces the drawings of various patterns for embroidery, white work and needle lace. It eloquently expounds upon the art and skill of contemporary needlework:

Thus plainely, and most truely is declar'd
The Needle workes hath still bin in regard,
For it doth ART, so like to NATURE frame,
As if IT were HER Sister, or the SAME.
Flowers, Plants, and Fishes, Beasts, Birds, Flyes & Bees,
Hils, Dales, Plaines, Pastures, Skies, Seas, Rivers, Trees:
There's nothing neare at hand, or farthest sought,
But with the Needle, may be shap'd or wrought.

This particularly beautiful example of a white work sampler has nine rows of carefully worked cut and drawn thread work with needlepoint fillings, similar to the designs in John Taylor's book.

17. Sampler made by C K, possibly south Germany, 1696

200.6 cm (6 ft 7 in.) x 48.9 cm (19 1/4 in.)

The majority of samplers in Glasgow Museums' collections are British, but this two-coloured sampler is probably a *stickmustertuch* from south Germany.

Although the sampler appears to be in the same band format as English samplers of this period, it is actually made from three separate pieces sewn together to create an exceptionally large sampler. It is worked using only cross and long-armed cross stitch rather than the wider variety of stitches found on seventeenth-century British samplers.

At the top is a depiction of the Sacred Heart pierced with arrows, a traditional symbol of Christ, shown beneath a crown and between two rampant lion supporters. Below is St George slaying the dragon. St George has been recognized as the patron saint of England since his adoption by Edward III in the fourteenth century, but from the time of the Crusades he was also seen throughout Christian Europe as the patron saint of soldiers.

The central section includes the Triumph of Christ surrounded by angels with the Lamb of God and a peacock below. Interestingly, this peacock is not as stylized as the two peacocks in the row above, which are very similar to the peacocks found on several Scottish samplers in the collection (see samplers 33, 39, 43 and 46), although all are depicted 'in pride' – with their tails open. Meandering at the bottom, on the smallest section of the sampler, is a procession headed by two heralds, and followed by figures and a coach drawn by four horses.

18. Sampler made by Jane Ann Terrill, England, circa 1700

81.9 cm (32 1/4 in.) x 20.3 cm (8 in.)

The patterns on this sampler are particularly bold, with the multicoloured silk threads still vivid after more than 300 years.

The bands chosen by Jane Ann Terrill are a mixture of those found on earlier seventeenth-century samplers, such as the poppies with twisted stems (see samplers 7, 13 and 15), the boxers (see samplers 6, 7 and 8), Florentine stitch (see sampler 1), and new ones. Amongst those which are new is the band with a pair of royal swans with crowns worked against a green ground, rather dominating this sampler (see detail below). At the bottom is a freely drawn tree with offshoots, contrasting with the more stylized motifs above. The centres of several of the flowers are embroidered with bullion knots.

19. Sampler made by Katy Wood, Scotland, 1739

31.4 cm (12 3/8 in.) x 21 cm (8 1/4 in.)

During the eighteenth century the shape and design of samplers began to change. The majority of early examples are long and thin, while later samplers are generally shorter and wider. This was because of the growing custom of framing the finished piece of needlework to display the skill of the young needleworker – this new size was easier to mount.

Katy Wood's sampler concentrates on letters, and whilst this would have served as a useful revision of the alphabet, their inclusion was more to do with practice for when she would have to mark all her household linen with family initials. The largest alphabet is sewn using eyelet stitch and has a flat-topped 'A' at the start – both common characteristics of Scottish samplers (see samplers 23, 30, 47 and 52). The use of red and green threads is also typically Scottish (see sampler 44).

The beginning of the eighteenth century saw a period of general stability throughout much of Great Britain. This resulted in the growth of the middle classes, whose social aspirations resulted in an increase in the education offered to their children. Samplers, already a mainstay of a girl's education, began to include religious and other moralizing texts, such as the Lord's Prayer at the bottom of this sampler, as a means of improving a child's behaviour and teaching Christian values. Here the maker has run out of space to complete the prayer.

ABCDEFGHIKLMNOPQRST
VWXYZ & ABCDEFGHIKL

abcdefghiklmnopqrstuuuu

ABCDEFGHIKLMNOPQRST
VWXYZ & ABCDEFGHIKL

Abcdefghiklmnopqrstuv
vw & Abcdefghiklmnopqrstuv

ABCDEFGHIKL

MNOPQRSTVW

XYZ & BCDE

ABCDEFGHIKLMNO

PQRSTVWXYZ & ABC
DEFGHIKLMNOPQRS

WW BIW XW XW MW XW
XFWWSWRBKW Wally Wood
Endedher sempler May 19 1739 123

The Lords   mercy Will be
prayer   done in earth as
Our Father Whi: it is in heaven gi:
ch Art in heave: ve us This day ou:
n Hallowed be t: r daily bread An
hy Kingdom co: d forgive us our

20. Sampler by Mrs Simpson, probably Scotland, 1765
29 cm (11 3/8 in.) x 19 cm (7 1/2 in.)

Made in the middle of the eighteenth century, this sampler combines elements from earlier band samplers with new developments. In the centre are two bold border patterns, including a large version of the poppies with twisted stems from the earlier tradition. Above these is a large alphabet with a flat-topped 'A' – marking it as probably Scottish – and missing not only its 'J' and 'U' but also its 'V'.

This sampler, worked on fine linen, is embroidered with a more limited range of stitches – cross, double running and satin – than those of a hundred years earlier. This reflects the subtle change from the sampler's main use in previous centuries as a record of different stitches to the classroom exercise that it would become in the nineteenth century.

The name at the bottom is hard to make out, but seems to imply the maker is a married woman. This is unusual, as the majority of samplers were made by children.

21. Sampler made by Susanna Orr, America, 1771

31.1 cm (12 1/4 in.) x 21.5 cm (8 1/2 in.)

This is a charming gift sampler, 'TO MR ROBERT ORR IN SCOTLAND FROM SUSANNA ORR IN AMERICA 1771'. The lozenge design of the body, worked in Florentine stitch, is reminiscent of Native American work. It is similar to another American piece, dated 1777, which was made into a pocketbook cover and is now in the Cooper Hewitt, National Design Museum, New York[1].

The distinctive shape with its two bottom corners cut off suggests that this sampler may have been made into a pouch, possibly to hold tobacco. During the eighteenth century Glasgow became the main British city importing tobacco from the American colonies and West Indies. Tobacco was sold in the form of loose dried leaves that were stored in small boxes or carried on the person in little bags and pouches. Mr Orr may have had his gift made into a pouch to remind him of its giver.

1. Illustrated in *The Needleworker's Dictionary*, p.35.

22. Sampler made by Jean Kerr, Glasgow, Scotland, circa 1802

45.7 cm (18 in.) x 58.4 cm (23 in.)

Samplers can serve as a record of various aspects of political, social and technological history. This one probably depicts its maker, Jean Kerr, on the left alongside her fashionably dressed mother and dashing father in his military uniform. The figures and the two large birds are in satin stitch with finer details in stem stitch.

When this sampler was made, Great Britain had been at war with France since 1793. Although the Peace of Amiens Treaty was signed in 1802, it was short-lived and the two sides were soon fighting again. During this period many volunteer regiments were formed, including a Regiment of Foot in Glasgow who trained hard in preparation for the feared invasion by the French by way of the River Clyde. However, the defeat of the French navy at the Battle of Trafalgar in 1805 ended Napoleon Bonaparte's ambition to conquer Britain, and he turned his attention to mainland Europe. The only action Glasgow's volunteers saw was when 300 of them were mustered in 1800 to protect Lord Campbell at Garscube from an angry mob rioting in protest at high taxes and unemployment.

The patriotic tone of this fine sampler is further reflected in the central medallion, where the initials 'GR' stand for *Georgius Rex* (King George), George III.

23. Sampler made by Janet Rankin, Glasgow, Scotland, 1809

44.1 cm (17 3/8 in.) x 40 cm (13 3/8 in.)

Many Scottish samplers provide a record of family history, as they often include the names or initials of the maker's family. From this sampler it is possible to deduce that Janet, the maker, was probably the eldest daughter of John Rankin and Janet Stirling, and she had seven siblings: William, Robert, John, Andrew, Elisabeth, Margaret and James. Sadly, it appears that her sister Elisabeth died young as her name is embroidered in black, the traditional colour of mourning. This method was generally adopted for the names of deceased relatives on Scottish samplers.

This is a particularly moral sampler, with biblical verses taken from Proverbs (31:30 and 8:17) and Luke (6:31). Excerpts from Proverbs were a popular choice, as their short verses were particularly suitable for use on samplers. Proverbs 31:3, 'Favour is deceitful and beauty is vain, but a woman that feareth the Lord she shall be praised', appears to have been a favourite as it is used here and on several other nineteenth-century samplers.

24. Sampler made in Great Britain, circa 1798–1829

42.5 cm (16 3/4 in.) x 66 cm (26 in.)

From the 1770s onwards, needlework maps were a popular form of sampler. This reflects European exploration and the spread of colonialism during the late eighteenth and early nineteenth centuries. Another map sampler in the collection dating from the 1770s bears the title 'The WORLD with all the MODERN DISCOVERIES', and shows the voyages of Captain James Cook, Captain Samuel Wallis (who discovered Tahiti), and Captain Philip Carteret (who discovered Pitcairn Island). Whilst the map pictured here does not show these specific expeditions, it does point out Owhyhee in the Sandwich Islands 'where Capt. Cook was killed 1779'. Australia is shown as New Holland, after the early Dutch explorers. Although Britain had colonized New South Wales in 1788, it did not claim the rest of Australia as a British territory until 1829.

This sampler, 'An outline MAP OF THE WORLD FOR LADIES NEEDLEWORK and Young Students in GEOGRAPHY, was 'Published by R. LAURIE & J. WHITTLE, No. 53 Fleet Street. Published as the Act directs January 1st 1798'. Richard Holmes Laurie and James Whittle were leading map and print sellers in London from 1794 until 1818, and were one of two London cartographers who produced maps printed on linen or silk for girls to embroider. New patterns were advertised in annual catalogues.

The anonymous embroiderer has sewn around the outlines of the continents in silk thread, using satin stitch.

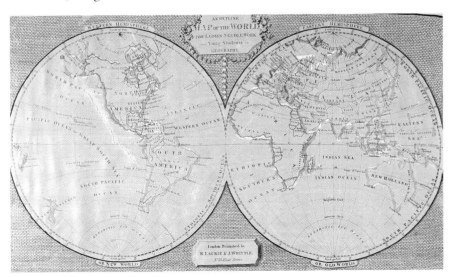

25. Sampler made by PR, Perth, Scotland, 1809

47 cm (18 1/2 in.) x 34.2 cm (13 1/2 in.)

Map samplers were a helpful method of learning geography. Interestingly, whilst several maps of England, Great Britain, Europe and the world have survived, individual maps of Scotland, Ireland or Wales are relatively rare. There is a Laurie & Whittle needlework map of Scotland in the National Library of Scotland.

This sampler is embroidered on wool canvas, with the outlines of the counties marked in various coloured silk threads. The double-headed eagle at the top, taken from the city of Perth's coat of arms, is worked in long and short stitches. On the right the North Sea is marked as the German Ocean, a term commonly used until the early nineteenth century.

Although we do not know who PR was, another sampler from the same source, made by Elizabeth Johnson in 1818, but without the double-headed eagle, also survives[1].

1. Illustrated in *Exceptional Endeavour*, p.38.

26. Sampler made by Margaret Wyllie, Glasgow, Scotland, 1820

50.2 cm (19 3/4 in.) x 43.1 cm (17 in.)

This map of early nineteenth-century Europe is much simpler than today's map, with Russia and Turkey dominating much of eastern Europe. However, Italy and Germany are misleadingly shown as single states – Italy was not unified until 1870 and Germany not until 1871.

Margaret Wyllie's sampler is worked on a fine wool canvas, embroidered in black and cream silk threads. An identical one in the collection was made in Glasgow by Janet Douglas about 1826, which suggests that this sampler may have been copied from a single source used by one particular teacher or school in Glasgow.

27. Sampler made by Margaret Sheddon, New Lanark School, Scotland, 1812

43.1 cm (17 in.) x 33.5 cm (13 1/8 in.)

Social reformer Robert Owen, the manager of the cotton mills at New Lanark, believed that a person's character was primarily the product of their environment. Not only was he against the employment of children under 12, but he also established a progressive school for children aged one to 12 with the aim:

> ... to give the children the most beneficial education for their station in the community, and effectually to train them to habits which could not fail to make them valuable members of society.

This wool sampler is a good example of his practical teaching. Beneath the initials of Robert Owen and his extended family, Margaret Sheddon has worked a row of crowns for a king, queen, prince, duke, marquess, earl, viscount, lord and baron. When a girl entered a royal or aristocratic household as a servant, one of her duties would be to sew the relevant crown and personal initials of her master or mistress onto all the household linen and family's undergarments. The name Agnes Richmond at the bottom of the sampler may be that of Margaret's teacher.

Margaret's father, William Sheddon, was the butler at Robert Owen's house at Broxfield, where her sister Mary was later a waiting maid for Charles Walker, Owen's successor.

Dancing class in the schoolroom at New Lanark, about 1825.

28. Sampler made by Bethulia Bonner, Great Britain, 1815
42.2 cm (16 5/8 in.) x 33.6 cm (13 1/4 in.)

The central motif on this sampler shows the Temptation of Adam and Eve. The unfortunate couple are standing beneath the Tree of Knowledge with the serpent between them encircling the trunk (see sampler 40). This depiction of man's first disobedience and fall from grace started to appear on samplers during the eighteenth century, and appears to have been particularly popular not only in Great Britain but also on the Continent.

The verse is a popular choice for samplers and probably dates from the late eighteenth century.

> Jesus Permit thy Gracious Name To
> Stand as the First Effort of An
> Infants Hand and While her fingers
> Over the Canvass move Engage her
> Tender Thoughts to Seek Thy love
> With thy Dear Children let her share
> Her Part and Write Thy Name
> Thyself Upon Her Hart

There are several versions of this poem. The earliest appears on the first American sampler, made by Loara Standish in the early 1640s (now in Pilgrim Hall Museum, Plymouth, Massachusetts). Loara was the daughter of Miles Standish who sailed on the *Mayflower* with the Pilgrim Fathers in 1620.

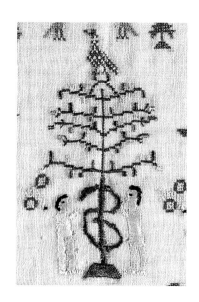

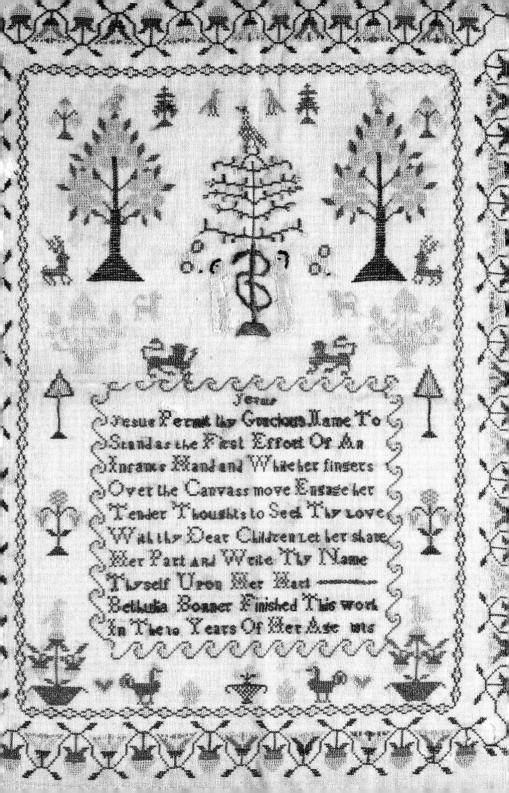

Jesus

Jesus Permit thy Gracious Name To
Stand as the First Effort Of An
Infants Hand and Whileher fingers
Over the Canvass move Engage her
Tender Thoughts to Seek Thy love
With thy Dear Children let her share
Her Part and Write Thy Name
Thyself Upon Her Hart ————
Bethula Bonner Finished This work
In The 10 Years Of Her Age 1815

29. Sampler made by Elizabeth Donald, Aberdeen, Scotland, 1811

53.2 cm (21 in.) x 33 cm (13 in.)

This is one of a small group of samplers in the collection that were made by three sisters, Elizabeth, Isabella and Katharine Donald (see samplers 30–32). They obviously copied their designs from the same source, possibly from a teacher at their school, as the samplers are all very similar.

Elizabeth appears to have been the eldest sister and this sampler is the earliest one of the set, dated 1811. The inclusion of family initials is typically Scottish, as is the use of eyelet stitch to work them. It is easy to deduce that 'AD' and 'KD' were Elizabeth's parents due to the prominence of these letters, whilst below are the initials of four siblings, including Isabella and Katharine. The absence of any samplers in the collection by siblings whose forenames begin with 'M' or 'A' suggests that 'MD and AD' may have been boys. The initials under the stag are probably those of members of the extended family.

30. Samplers made by Isabella and Katharine Donald, Aberdeen, Scotland, 1814 & 1820

43.1 cm (17 in.) x 32.4 cm (12 3/4 in.); 54 cm (21 1/4 in.) x 35.5 cm (14 in.)

Katharine Donald's sampler is nearly identical to one embroidered six years earlier by her older sister Isabella (see below right). The composition is similar, with the rows of border patterns and alphabets at the top, initials in the middle, and a selection of motifs at the bottom, including the same simple façade of a house.

Interestingly, one of the main differences is Isabella's use of her mother's maiden initials, 'KI', in the centre of the sampler. For several centuries it was customary for married women in Scotland to use their maiden name as well as their married name. With the current interest in tracing family history, several people are turning to old family samplers to assist with their hunt, and this earlier tradition of married women keeping their father's name is proving to be helpful when tracing maternal lines.

31. Sampler made by Isabella Donald, Aberdeen, Scotland, 1817

23.6 cm (9 1/4 in.) x 21.3 cm (8 1/4 in.)

When contrasted with her sampler of three years earlier, Isabella Donald's second surviving sampler shows how her needlework improved with age and practice. This is also the most advanced sampler made by any of the three sisters.

Again, the overall design and individual motifs have been copied from the same source as the sisters' earlier samplers. The border pattern with repeated strawberries appears on several other Scottish samplers, including not only these by the Donald sisters (see samplers 29–30), but also one by Janet Milne, Glasgow, dated 1831 (see sampler 47). Underneath are the parents' initials in cross stitch, with finely drawn detailing carefully worked in back stitch.

In the lower half, reminiscent of seventeenth-century spot motif samplers (see sampler 1), are a range of simple motifs scattered randomly across the ground to fill the space, including the bird found on her earlier sampler.

32. Samplers probably made by Isabella Donald, Aberdeen, Scotland, circa 1820

13.5 cm (5 3/4 in). x 11.8 cm (4 1/2 in.); 10.2 cm (4 1/4 in.) x 10.2 (4 1/4 in.)

Isabella appears to have been the Donald sister most accomplished at needlework, as can be seen by the neatness of her earlier samplers (see samplers 30 and 31). It is therefore probable that she made these two delightful specimens.

Both are fairly small, and worked on cotton with precise, tiny cross stitches in multi-coloured silk threads. The variety of small motifs are more naturalistically drawn than those found on the other sisters' samplers.

The second piece also includes bands of simple drawn thread work between the lines of a verse. The message suggests that Isabella may have worked these two examples as small gifts for members of her family.

33. Sampler made by Janet McNiel, Scotland, 1819

44.1 cm (17 3/4 in.) x 33.5 cm (13 1/4 in.)

Janet McNiel's sampler is characteristic of Scottish samplers of the nineteenth century. Along the top is the popular poppy border with its twisted stems that survived from the early band samplers (see sampler 7). A simplified version of this has been used as the border. Below is the row of crowns in practice for sewing monograms on household linen. In the centre is a moral verse taken from a 1709 hymn by Bishop Thomas Ken, a popular choice for samplers.

At the bottom, the large, boldly drawn building is a version of the standardized schoolhouse that appears on many samplers. It has a gable-topped central building flanked by a small wing on each side. Scottish examples such as this often have striking blue roofs (perhaps to reflect the roof slates) and a front lawn stitched in three shades of green chenille thread. On the top of the gable, like a weathervane, is the open-tailed peacock that is found on so many Scottish samplers.

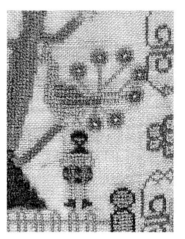

Almost hidden from view in the lower corners are two small black boys. These may be representations of the black servants it was fashionable to have during the eighteenth and early nineteenth centuries. Often they were dressed in elaborate uniforms to signify their master's wealth, especially if derived from large plantations in the Caribbean and America. Although British involvement in the slave trade was abolished in 1807, many slaves and bonded servants were not granted their freedom until 1833.

34. *Sampler from* A Model of the System of Teaching Needlework in the Elementary Schools of the British and Foreign School Society, *Great Britain, 1821*

17.8 cm (7 in.) x 11.8 cm (4 1/2 in.)

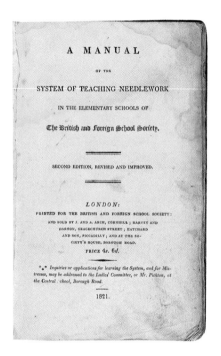

The British and Foreign School Society was founded by Joseph Lancaster in 1808 'for the purpose of affording education, procuring employment and as far as possible to furnish clothing to the children of the poorer subjects of King George III'. The initial aim of the Society was to encourage the foundation of schools in Britain. However, its influence was widespread and in 1816 the first *Manual for the Model School* was published to great success and was soon translated into many languages. It was followed by several textbooks including this needlework manual (see left), so popular that in 1821 it was already into its second edition. The manual was published with 35 pages of printed instructions outlining timetable, manner of behaviour, method of teaching and types of needlework, together with blank pages for students' finished samplers to be added.

This book came from the Model School at Kildare Place, Dublin. The Kildare Place Society, Dublin (also known as The Society for Promoting the Education of the Poor in Ireland) was established in 1811 through the efforts of John Foster, Chancellor of the Exchequer for Ireland. In 1816 it established Model Schools in Dublin, followed by further schools throughout Ireland. Inside the book are over 20 examples of needlework showing the progress from hemming in the first class to completed samplers made by the 10th class in 1827, and by Eliza Wright of the 10th class in 1829. Also included is this sampler by the Finishing Class, in wool canvas embroidered in polychrome silk threads, dated 1825.

35. Sampler made by Martha Pollard, Ackworth School, Yorkshire, England, 1811

46 cm (18 1/8 in.) x 54 cm (21 1/4 in.)

Ackworth School is a Quaker school founded by John Fothergill and others in 1779 for the education of 'Children of Friends not in affluence'. In the nineteenth century, all children were taught English language, writing and arithmetic, whilst girls were also taught 'Housewifry and useful needlework'. In 1778 Dr Fothergill wrote in a 'Letter to a Friend in the Country' that his aim:

> To habituate children from early infancy, at stated times, to silence and attention, is of the greater advantage to them, not only as a means of their making real advances in a religious life, but as the groundwork of the greater human prudence.

The octagon, or eight-sided, medallion form appears on several other samplers made by pupils from Ackworth School, including one by Frances Rae made in 1797[1] and one by Hannah Willis from 1802[2]. In some cases a single medallion has been made up into a pincushion. This design seems to have been particularly favoured by Quaker schools both in England and America, as it is also found on samplers made by pupils at Society of Friends' schools in Westtown, Pennsylvania, and Nine Partners, New York.

Martha Pollard was a pupil at Ackworth School from 1809 to 1811. It was the custom of girls leaving Ackworth School to make parting gifts for their friends or teachers. This sampler, made as 'a token of love' by Martha, was probably such a gift.

Ackworth School today.

1. Illustrated in *Samplers*, p.122.
2. Illustrated in *Diligence, Industry and Virtue*, p.26.

M Pollard

A TOKEN OF LOVE 1811

36. Sampler made at Ackworth School, Yorkshire, England, 1826

36.5 cm (14 3/8 in.) x 21 cm (8 1/4 in.)

Handwritten on the reverse of this sampler is the inscription 'Specimens of darning Ackworth School 1826'. There is a similar, smaller darning sampler made by Margaret Boxall in the collection at Ackworth School. Margaret Boxall was a pupil at Ackworth between 1793 and 1799. Her sampler has a note on the back stating:

> Such girls as choose to have one of these work them in play hours as it is thought it would take up too much time to do them in School, having other pieces to work, as well as their own and the household linen to make and mend.

These 'other pieces to work' were part of the manual work that was combined with the education that every child received. The pupils were known locally as good at plain sewing. Many took orders to make children's bed linen to help raise funds for the school besides making those for the school's use. Initially children were sent to Ackworth for the duration of their education and did not return home until this was finished. It was not until 1847 that the school instituted annual holidays.

Today, Ackworth School has 580 pupils and is one of only eight Quaker schools still open in Great Britain.

37. Sampler made by Priscilla Dell, Ackworth School, Yorkshire, England, 1826

19 cm (7 1/2 in.) x 19.5 cm (7 3/4 in.)

Fine muslin and silk gauze dresses were the height of fashion from the last decade of the eighteenth century until the 1820s. The delicacy of muslin and silk gauze was particularly suited to the elegant neoclassical gowns of the Directoire, Empire and Regency periods with their flowing lines, but the looseness of the weave of these materials meant that threads were easily caught, or worse, torn.

This sampler, worked by Priscilla Dell, demonstrates four darning patterns that use threads pulled from the edge of the muslin. These techniques could be used when mending the sheer muslin dresses. Several of the Regency flowered muslin dresses in Glasgow Museums' collection suffered small tears and have been mended by some neat hand at the time. Interestingly, repairs made later when these garments were worn as items of fancy dress are rather clumsy in comparison, reflecting the fact that later generations did not learn how to darn by making samplers such as this.

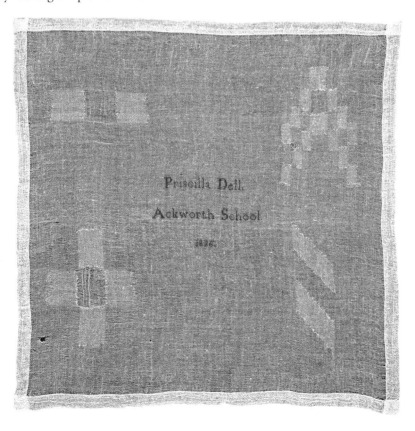

38. Sampler made by Priscilla Dell, Ackworth School, Yorkshire, England, 1827

34.7 cm (13 3/4 in.) x 27 cm (10 5/8 in.)

The second sampler in the collection by Priscilla Dell is one of a number from Ackworth School that include a verse or passage within a simple oval line border. This one, made during Priscilla's final year at Ackworth, is of the popular verse 'Solitude'. Identical samplers made by other pupils are still in the school's collection.

Other Ackworth samplers with verses on 'Religion' or 'Virtue' survive, such as the example worked by Emma Palmer in 1833[1]. These samplers were usually on wool canvas, embroidered in one colour in cross stitch for the verse and chain stitch for the border.

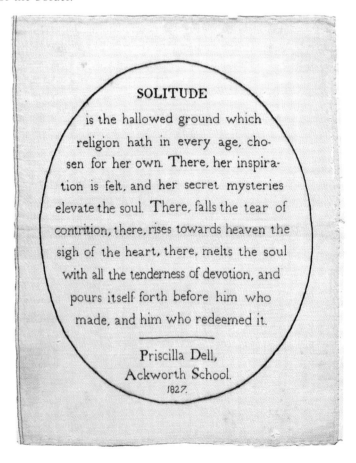

1.Illustrated in *Diligence, Industry and Virtue*, p.43.

39. Sampler made by Elisabeth V Vidal, Scotland, 1824

32 cm (12 5/8 in.) x 32.4 cm (12 3/4 in.)

This charming sampler by Elisabeth Vidal makes use of several traditional motifs that have changed little since the early seventeenth century. Along the top is a clear example of the flower border with twisted stems that was particularly popular in Scotland. This continued to be used on samplers well into the nineteenth century, long after the pattern had gone out of fashion in England (see samplers 7, 13, 15 and 18). Arranged symmetrically below is a series of motifs including vases of flowers and a pair of peacocks with their tails open and eyes clearly marked.

Although Elizabeth has not stated where she made the sampler, the combination of these particular motifs and border patterns is typically Scottish.

40. Sampler made by Robina Story, Scotland, circa 1820–1840

33 cm (13 in.) x 32.5 cm (12 3/4 in.)

Robina Story's sampler is peculiarly old-fashioned with its composition reminiscent of seventeenth-century spot samplers (see samplers 1 and 4). Several of the motifs are very similar to those seen on earlier band samplers, including the two stylized floral squares that can be seen in the top right. Amongst the large designs is one showing Adam and Eve standing beneath the Tree of Knowledge with an S-shaped snake between them (see also sampler 28), while another shows a crowned thistle within an octagonal border (see also sampler 41).

This sampler is also unusual for its date as it still retains a variety of stitches such as chain, running, satin and tent, as well as the almost mandatory cross stitch. This was the mainstay of nineteenth-century samplers, and in many cases was the only stitch used. Indeed the cross stitch has become so inextricably linked with samplers that the majority of kits available for today's needleworkers, whether whole samplers or individual motifs, invariably use only the cross stitch.

41. Sampler made by Jessie Henderson, Edinburgh, Scotland, circa 1820–1840

49.5 cm (19 5/8 in.) x 31.7 cm (12 1/2 in.)

Many of the buildings on samplers are generic designs, but the one featured on this sampler has been identified as the façade of the Orphan School of Edinburgh. During the eighteenth and nineteenth centuries several schools were set up to educate orphans and children from poorer families. Without a family, dowry or prospects, it was especially important for pupils to acquire useful skills in preparation for their future employment as maids, seamstresses or teachers. The making of samplers and other similar items of needlework seems to have played a particularly important role in the education of young girls.

Elements of this busy sampler include the teacher's name, Miss Catherine Gibson, and other initials. These are probably not of Jessie's family members, but are possibly those of her surrogate family – the other pupils of the school and teachers or governors. There are verses from an unfinished version of the Ten Commandments and the Book of Revelation (12:13), the latter forming part of the service for the Burial of the Dead from the *Book of Common Prayer*. In the bottom left corner is an octagonal (8-sided) motif with a crowned thistle in the centre and the motto 'I have power to defend myself and others' around it. Whilst the origin of the thistle is unknown, it has been found on several other Scottish samplers (see sampler 40).

Made of fine wool canvas, the sampler is worked using a variety of stitches including back, cross, running, satin, and tent stitches. However, the date of when it was made has been unpicked – possibly by Jessie later in life to hide her age from family and friends.

42. Sampler made by Ann Limbird, Bisham School, Berkshire, England, 1827

41.5 cm (16 3/4 in.) x 28 cm (11 in.)

Bisham School in Berkshire, England, was founded in 1786 to teach 20 poor local girls how to sew. The school was originally housed in a fifteenth-century manor house on land given in the late eighteenth century by members of the Vansittart family who owned the Bisham Abbey Estate. By the early nineteenth century the curriculum had expanded and boys were admitted.

This sampler is more typically English, with more exposed ground material than those made in Scotland (see sampler 49). The biblical text is from Philippians (4:6–7), and the verse from a hymn by Sir Robert Grant:

An Hymn
WHEN gath'ring clouds around I view,
And days are dark, and friends are few,
On him I lean, who not in vain
Experienc'd ev'ry human pain
He sees my griefs allays my fears,
And counts and treasures up my tears.

The building at the bottom may be generic rather than an actual depiction of Ann's own school. The heads of two angelic beings can clearly be seen on the roof, but it is uncertain what they signify.

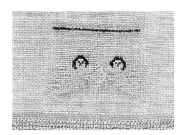

Be careful for nothing, but in every thing by
prayer and supplication with thanksgiving
let your requests be made known unto God
And the peace of God which passeth all
understanding, shall keep your hearts and
minds through CHRIST JESUS.

Phil. IV. 6.7.

An Hymn

WHEN gath'ring clouds around I view,
And days are dark, and friends are few;
On him I lean, who not in vain
Experienc'd ev'ry human pain:
He sees my griefs allays my fears,
And counts and treasures up my tears.

Done at the Bisham School by Ann Limbird Aged 12 Years 1827

43. Sampler made by Jane Hall, Scotland, 1827

42.5 cm (16 3/4 in.) x 31.7 cm (12 1/2 in.)

From the names at the top of this sampler it is possible to work out that Jane Hall was the daughter of William Hall and Ann Caroline Walker. Within the family, Jane may also have gone by the name of Jean, as another sampler donated to the collection at the same time has the inscription 'Jean Hall age 8 1823'.

During the 1850s Jane was employed by Margaret Bryce Gray to care for Margaret's invalid daughter. The daughter later inherited not only her mother's sampler, made in 1833 when she was seven, but also the two samplers by Jane/Jean Hall.

The main section of this typically Scottish sampler, with its inclusion of Jane's mother's maiden name and peacocks in pride, is embroidered in cross stitch. The verse was a popular choice for samplers (see also sampler 28); however, the flower and foliage border appears to have been embroidered at a later date. Worked in chain, leaf and satin stitches, its design is much freer than that found on many samplers, and the quality of the needlework is rather clumsy in places.

44. Sampler made by Margaret Stewart, Dunkeld, Scotland, 1830

43.1 cm (17 in.) x 21.8 cm (8 1/2 in.)

Many examples of simple samplers such as this survive. They were the first samplers young girls would make when they were about five or six years old. Margaret Stewart was six when she completed this in 1830.

Margaret's first sampler is very typical of those made in Scotland during the late eighteenth and early nineteenth centuries. This, like several others in the collection and throughout the country, reflects the Scottish preference for using predominantly red and green silk or wool threads. These relatively uncomplicated samplers were worked on plain weave, or tabby, linen with rows of alphabets and numerals. Only the easiest, decorative lines between were worked in simple cross stitch.

Over the following three years, Margaret's needlework skills would become more advanced as she developed the manual dexterity required to sew more delicate and complicated designs (see samplers 45 and 46).

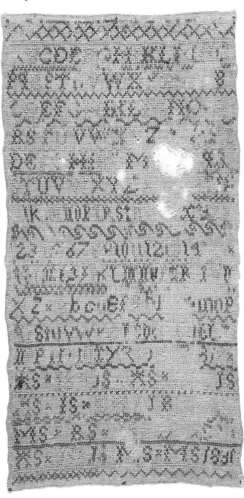

45. Sampler made by Margaret Stewart, Dunkeld, Scotland, 1832

23 cm (9 in.) x 22.8 cm (9 in.)

By the age of eight Margaret Stewart's needlework skills progressed (see sampler 44) to the extent that she was able to complete this very neat monochrome multiplication sampler.

There are various examples of samplers being used to teach subjects such as mathematics and geography. Multiplication tables appear to have been popular in Scotland. They are generally quite plain, although a few surviving examples have more complicated and elaborate borders, such as one made by Jean Miller in 1825[1].

Margaret's table appears to be based on a widely available source, as other identical samplers survive, including one made by a rather precocious Catherine Walker who was only six when she finished hers in about 1800[2].

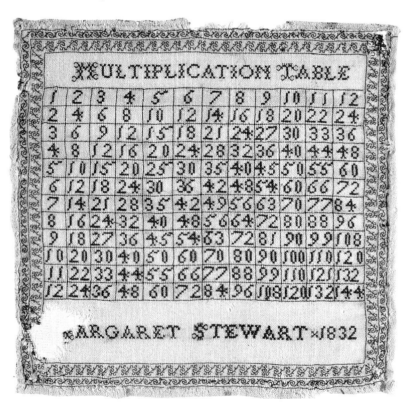

1. Illustrated in *Samplers*, p.121.
2. Now owned by the Duke of Atholl and illustrated in *Scottish Embroidery*, p.108.

46. Sampler made by Margaret Stewart, Dunkeld, Scotland, 1833

48.9 cm (19 1/4 in.) x 46.8 cm (18 3/4 in.)

Having mastered not only needlework skills in the course of three years, but also the necessary patience, Margaret Stewart completed her most decorative sampler in 1833 (see samplers 44 and 45). Whereas first samplers were not mounted, later samplers such as this generally were framed, and hung on school or nursery walls as examples of good work and accomplishment.

The survival of a set of samplers by the same maker is quite unusual. It provides a useful guide to the stages in which girls were taught embroidery, and the development of their skills over these formative years. People are always impressed at the quality of the work produced by these young girls. How many of today's nine-year-olds would be able to sit down and complete something like this?

47. Sampler made by Janet Milne, Glasgow, Scotland, 1831

50.7 cm (20 in.) x 42 cm (16 1/2 in.)

Janet was the second daughter of Alexander Milne, whose name is embroidered on the left along with the names of other relations. For some reason she has not included that of her older sister Christine, whose sampler is also in the collection. Mr Milne was a plantation owner who had retired from Jamaica with his family to Gartferry House in Chryston, near Glasgow. The family's connection to Nicholson Street Chapel in Laurieston is not known, unfortunately.

This sampler combines several elements found on other Scottish samplers in the collection. One of the alphabets is worked in eyelet stitch, while another starts with a flat-topped 'A' (see also sampler 19) and has fine curls worked in back stitch around each letter (see also sampler 31). The strawberry border pattern and the stylized vase, or urn, with five flowers including a central tulip worked in cross stitch, are also found on samplers made by the Donald sisters of Aberdeen (see samplers 29–31), suggesting that these were copied from a source that was available across Scotland.

48. Sampler made by Margaret Stewart, Alloa, Scotland, 1832

42.2 cm (16 5/8 in.) x 32 cm (12 5/8 in.)

The church depicted here, with its striking blue roof, is St Mungo's Parish Church in Alloa. It was designed by James Gillespie Graham and built in 1819 in the Scottish Gothic style that was becoming fashionable at this period. Its inclusion may indicate that this sampler was made to commemorate a special occasion, such as a wedding. The initials JJC and WS may be those of the bride and groom.

Margaret Stewart made it when she was 16, probably during her leisure hours rather than as part of her education. Several English samplers include important buildings such as churches and castles that were local to the maker, so Margaret may have included the church as a significant landmark.

Today, the church's tall steeple is still a feature of the neighbourhood.

49. Sampler made by Elizabeth Yuile, probably England, 1838

39.6 cm (15 5/8 in.) x 33 cm (13 in.)

Elizabeth's sampler is more typical of nineteenth-century English samplers (see sampler 42). Whilst these often featured the maker's name, they rarely included the names or initials of family names as can be found on Scottish samplers. The design of English samplers is often plainer too. Areas of ground material are left unworked which on a Scottish sampler might have been filled with an additional motif, and a slightly more uniform approach taken for the borders and motifs.

The main focus of the sampler is the poem 'On Contentment', worked in cross stitch in silk thread, as are the surrounding motifs and border. However, the main door of what appears to be quite an ordinary house has been embellished with a picot loop for its doorknocker and a bullion knot for its handle.

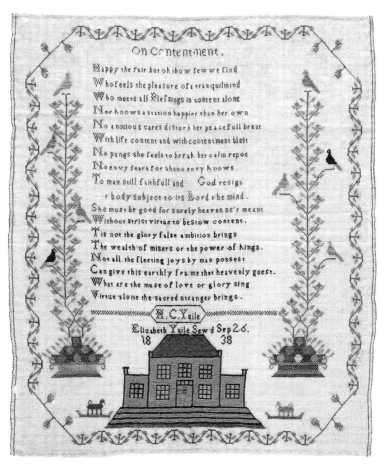

50. Sampler made by Elizabeth Smith, Scotland, 1839

53.7 cm (21 1/8 in.) x 51.5 cm (20 1/4 in.)

As so many samplers were embroidered as part of girls' formal education, it is not surprising that school buildings are often prominent. In some cases these can be identified as specific buildings (see sampler 41), while others show what appears to be a very stereotypical school (see sampler 33). This is what is depicted here, with its vibrant blue gabled roof.

Although Elizabeth does not say where her school was, we can guess that her teachers were probably the Revd Dr Beattie and his wife as their names are embroidered on the right. On the left are the names of Elizabeth's parents – John Smith, whose early death is marked by the use of black silk to embroider his name, and Mary Ann Woolley. The initials below are those of Elizabeth's siblings and extended family.

Evenly scattered over most of the wool ground is a variety of motifs, leaving little space uncovered. Many are embroidered solely in cross stitch, but the larger arrangements of flowers at the top and on either side of the building have been freely embroidered using cross, satin and stem stitches. The difference in technique and design suggests that these may have been added at a later date (see sampler 43).

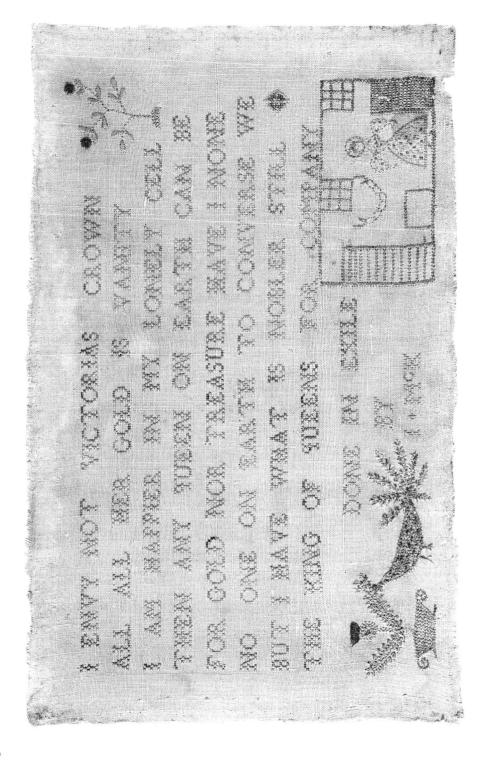

51. Sampler made by I McK, Great Britain, circa 1837–1840

19 cm (7 1/2 in.) x 30 cm (11 3/4 in.)

A female prisoner made this unusual sampler – 'Done in Exile'. Although it is not known exactly where or when it was made, the initials 'I McK', the inclusion of the thistles, and the use of 'we' for 'with' suggest that the maker was Scottish.

Originally jails were privately run, but in 1823 Sir Robert Peel introduced his Prison Reform Bill. However, the improvements set out in this Bill did not apply to debtors' prisons, and conditions in local town jails continued to be bad. Elizabeth Fry, a Quaker, was shocked by the state of the British penal system. She visited many jails around the country, including those in Aberdeen and Glasgow, as part of her campaign for further reforms.

During the 1830s and 1840s all prisoners awaiting transportation to British penal colonies were imprisoned in London. Elizabeth Fry visited the female prisoners, giving them material and sewing equipment. This was to enable them to make a quilt on the voyage, either to sell at their destination or to demonstrate their skill to potential employers once freed.

The woman's dress at the bottom of the sampler, with its large leg-of-mutton sleeves, reflects the fashions of the early 1830s, but the reference to Queen Victoria points to a date post-1837. The earlier style may recall the fashions when I McK was first imprisoned, or the dated fashions found in a colony if she was exiled abroad.

Elizabeth Fry reading to the prisoners at Newgate, 1816.

52. Sampler made by Elizabeth Nicholson, Scotland, 1842

39 cm (15 3/8 in.) x 42.5 cm (16 3/4 in.)

The dogs and roses embroidered at the bottom of this sampler are examples of Berlin wool work. As the name suggests, this originated in Berlin in 1804 when Phillipson, a publisher, printed 12 hand-coloured patterns for cross stitch embroidery. However, it was not until 1831 that a London publisher started to sell a large number of similar designs that he had purchased in Berlin. The craze for Berlin wool work soon spread, and by 1840 over 14,000 brightly coloured designs had been published. During the next 20 years these embroidery patterns became the height of fashion across Britain, Europe and America.

As well as being highly coloured, these designs were more naturalistic than the motifs found on earlier samplers, and increasingly reflected the Victorian love of sentimental subjects. Although initially designed for cross stitch, many patterns were worked on canvas and decorated household items from slippers to cushions. Along with biblical and historical scenes, often copied from pictures by artists such as Sir Edwin Henry Landseer, two of the more popular subjects were flowers and dogs, especially the royal canines. Amongst the examples of Berlin wool work pictures in the collection are depictions of Mary, Queen of Scots after the Battle of Langside, and Queen Victoria's dogs.

53. Sampler made in Great Britain, mid-19th century

78 cm (30 3/4 in.) x 14.6 cm (5 3/4 in.)

The long narrow shape of this canvas work sampler is in the tradition of seventeenth-century band samplers. Less decorative than other samplers of the period, it was probably worked by an adult as a reference or practice piece and would have been stored rolled up in her workbox rather than framed as an example of her accomplishments.

Every tenth warp thread in the canvas ground is dyed yellow, which must have helped the embroiderer count her stitches. The geometric motifs are embroidered in a wider variety of stitches than those found on children's samplers of the period, and include cross, Florentine and satin stitches, reflecting the use of this sampler as a stitch and pattern guide.

A few of the embroidered designs are decorated with faceted gilt steel beads, which were a novelty during this period. In 1854 Sir Henry Bessemer patented his de-carbonization process for mass-manufacturing steel from pig iron. As well as being put to a wide range of commercial and manufacturing uses, steel was adopted by the fashion industry, most noticeably for the new cage-crinolines introduced in 1856. Another use was in the creation of a range of decorative items such as buckles, buttons and beads, as cut steel was a cheaper alternative to silver. These beads have become tarnished over time, as the steel at this date was not stainless, but when new they would have glittered as they caught the light.

54. Miniature shirt made by Catherine Bayne, Gray Abbey School, County Down, Ireland, circa 1850–1853

23 cm (9 1/4 in.) x 41.5 cm (16 1/4 in.)

A new form of sampler began to appear in the middle of the nineteenth century. This was partly as a result of the huge changes in society caused by the growth of industry and the accompanying movement away from agriculture and rural ways of living. Many children were now educated with a view to their future employment, not just as a sign of their parents' wealth and social status (real or aspiring). Needlework skills were seen not solely as the domain of accomplished ladies, but as a means of employment for many working- and lower middle-class women. The emphasis in teaching began to switch from decorative needlework towards plain sewing, covering how to make and mend basic garments.

One of the most common methods of this new form of teaching was for pupils to make small examples of clothing, such as this miniature shirt made by Catherine Bayne. Catherine had been abandoned as a baby, but was adopted by a local family. She was sent to Gray Abbey School in County Down to be educated, where she won first prize with this shirt. It was probably a useful reference for her when she left school in about 1854, aged 12, and found employment as a lady's maid to the 11-year-old Lady Helen Laura MacDonnell, only daughter of the 9th Earl of Antrim. Catherine rose to the rank of Lady Helen's housekeeper, and remained in service with the family until her death in 1919.

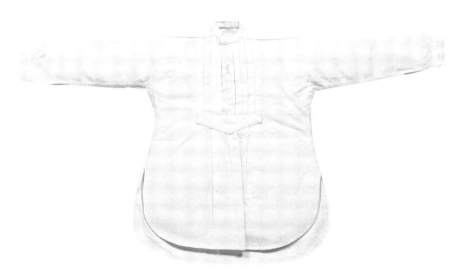

55. Sampler made by Jessie Goldie, Drybridge School, 1864

51.7 cm (20 3/8 in.) x 43.1 cm (17 in.)

One of the major discoveries of the nineteenth century was man-made dye. Before this, natural sources such as plants or animal products were used to make the colours. Those that could produce strong, long-lasting colours were extremely expensive. Cochineal, a red dye made from crushed beetles, required approximately 17,000 insects to produce one ounce of dye.

The first synthetic aniline dye was discovered by the Prussian chemist Otto Unverdorben in 1826, after he heated and distilled the natural blue dye indigo (the name aniline comes from *anil*, the Spanish word for indigo). However, it was not until William Henry Perkins' discovery of mauve dye in 1856, which he successfully patented and produced commercially, that synthetic dyes began to be used widely. Within the next ten years brilliant new shades of purple, pink and green dyes became available for clothing and needlework. One of the better-known early synthetic dyes was fuschine, discovered by François-Emmanuel Verguin in 1858, and named after the flower fuchsia. Other companies produced variations of this dye, and as the dye was used commonly for military uniforms, its different names often derive from famous battles. Magenta is named after Garibaldi's victory in north Italy in 1859, and solferino after a battle during the Franco-Piedmontese war against Austria.

Several of these new dyes were used to produce the striking colours of the wools used by Jessie Goldie on this sampler. As well as increasing the range of colours and shades, aniline dyes were more affordable as they could be derived from the cheap by-products of other industries.

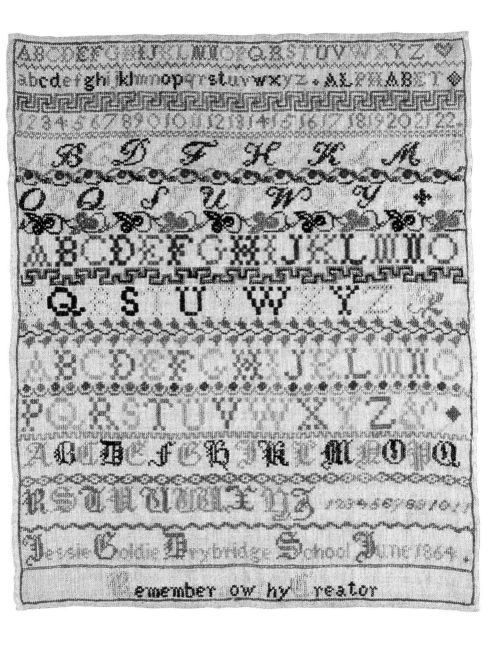

56. Miniature bodice and skirt, made in Glasgow, Scotland, 1900

76.1 cm (30 in.) x 47 cm (18 1/2 in.)

Several miniature garments in the collection date from the early twentieth century. Most were made by girls in the final stages of their education at the specialist domestic science colleges that had opened up in Glasgow and other major cities. As well as plain sewing techniques, such as different styles of hems, pin tucks, and buttonholes, pupils were taught basic pattern cutting skills, including those for underwear and dresses.

This miniature dress, consisting of bodice and skirt in navy blue wool, is an exact replica of a full-sized everyday outfit worn in 1900. Everything is correctly made, but on a small scale. The bodice has the high standing collar and fitted body of the period, complete with fastenings of blue buttons, lining and small blue silk-covered bones. The skirt is made with long, gored panels and lined with glazed cotton. The braid sewn around the hem of the skirt protects it from wear.

These dressmaking samplers formed part of a student's portfolio, and assisted them in finding work in one of the dressmaking establishments in Glasgow. The large department stores, such as Copland and Lye, sold ready-made garments and employed large numbers of seamstresses to alter their made-to-measure ranges or fulfil bespoke orders. There were also numerous independent dressmakers scattered across the city.

57. Sampler by Mary Thomson, Glasgow, 1903

55.8 cm (22 in.) x 38.1 cm (15 in.)

Mary Thomson's sampler is the most recent sampler acquired for the collection and has definite ties to Glasgow. Mary was born on 26 May 1884 and was a pupil at Kent Road School in Glasgow, which opened in 1886. She later became a pupil teacher there, and it was probably during this period that she made this sampler with its 21 examples of plain sewing techniques. The sampler was exhibited in Glasgow in 1903.

Mary went on to study at the University of Glasgow, which was still relatively rare for women, and graduated with a First Class degree in French and German. She then returned to teaching, taking a post at the Glasgow High School for Girls. As was the custom, Mary retired from teaching upon her marriage to Francis CH Mackenzie in 1921, and settled in Edinburgh.

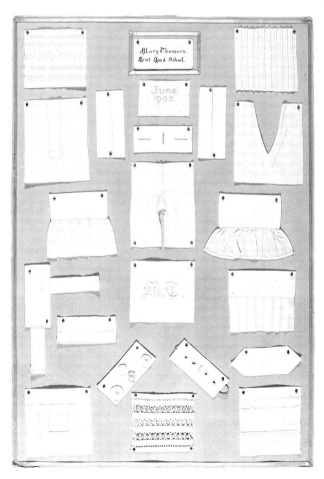

Chronology

1597 John Gerald's *Herbal or General History Plants* published

1603 Accession of James IV as James I

1620 Pilgrim Fathers sail to America aboard the *Mayflower*

1625 Accession of Charles I

1631 John Taylor's *The Needles Excellency* published

1633 Thomas Johnson's revised *Herbal* published

1642 Beginning of the Civil War   Judith Fisher c.1640s

1649 Execution of Charles I; foundation of the Commonwealth

1651 Battle of Worcester and escape of Charles II to France

1658 Death of Cromwell

1660 Restoration of Charles II

1662 Marriage of Charles II and   A Austen 1663
Catherine of Branganza   Frances Cheyney 1663, 1664
                                             Elizabeth Fares 1664
                                             Jane Turner 1668

1673 Marriage of James, Duke of York,
and Mary of Modena   Elizabeth Priest 1674

1685 Accession of James II

1688 Glorious Revolution; James II deposed and exiled

1689 Accession of William III and Mary II

1701 Act of Settlement   Jane Ann Terrill c.1700

1702 Accession of Queen Anne

1707 Act of Union

1714	Accession of George I	
1727	Accession of George II	
		Katy Wood 1739
1760	Accession of George III	Susanna Orr 1771
1779	*Olney Hymns* published; Ackworth School, Yorkshire, founded	
1786	Bisham School, Berkshire, founded	
1807	Abolition of slavery	
1808	British and Foreign School Society founded	Janet Rankin 1809 Martha Pollard 1811 Margaret Sheddon 1812 Janet McNiel 1819
1820	Accession of George IV	Margaret Wyllie 1820
1821	*Manual for the System of Teaching Needlework in the Elementary Schools of the British and Foreign School Society* published	Elizabeth Vidal 1824 Model School Kildare Place 1825 Priscilla Dell 1826, 1827 Ann Limbird 1827 Jane Hall 1827
1830	Accession of William IV	Margaret Stewart 1830, 1832, 1833 Janet Milne 1831
1837	Accession of Victoria	Elizabeth Yuile 1838 Elizabeth Smith 1839 Elizabeth Nicolson 1842
1854	Henry Bessemer patents a process for making steel	
1856	William Perkins patents the first aniline dye	Jessie Goldie 1864
1872	Education Act establishes School Boards in Scotland	
1901	Accession of Edward VII	Mary Thompson 1903
1906	Scotland Street School, Glasgow, opens	

Catalogue information

1. Sampler made in England, c.1625–1630
Silk and silver threads on linen
52 cm x 33.6 cm (20 1/2 in. x 13 1/4 in.)
Glasgow Museums, Burrell Collection 31.1

2. Sampler made in England, c.1630–1650
Silk and silver threads on linen
52.7 cm x 26 cm (20 3/4 in. x 10 1/4 in.)
Glasgow Museums, Burrell Collection 31.6

3. White work sampler made by Judith Fisher, England, c.1640
Silk threads on linen
25.4 cm x 22.8 cm (10 in. x 9 in.)
Glasgow Museums, Burrell Collection 31.13

4. Sampler made in England, mid-17th century
Silk threads on linen
43.1 cm x 58.4 cm (17 in. x 23 in.)
Glasgow Museums, Burrell Collection 31.10

5. Sampler made in England, mid-17th century
Silk threads on linen
94.6 cm x 17.8 cm (37 1/4 in. x 7 in.)
Glasgow Museums, Burrell Collection 31.7

Detail: Needlework casket, late 17th century, Glasgow Museums, Burrell Collection 29.165

6. Sampler made in England, mid-17th century
Silk threads on linen
92.7 cm x 18.4 cm (36 1/2 in. x 7 1/4 in.)
Glasgow Museums, Burrell Collection 31.9

Detail: Embroidered black work border on a pillowcase, Glasgow Museums, Burrell Collection 29.235

7. Sampler made in England, mid-17th century
Silk threads on linen
90.1 cm x 17.8 cm (35 1/2 in. x 7 in.)
Glasgow Museums, Burrell Collection 31.3

8. Sampler made in England, mid-17th century
Silk threads on linen
104.1 cm x 20.3 cm (41 in. x 8 in.)
Glasgow Museums, Burrell Collection 31.17

9. Sampler made in England, mid-17th century
Linen threads on linen
74.9 cm x 14 cm (29 1/2 in. x 5 1/2 in.)
Glasgow Museums, Burrell Collection 31.14

10. Sampler made by A Austen, Great Britain, 1663
Silk threads on linen
74.2 cm x 17.1 cm (29 1/4 in. x 6 3/4 in.)
Glasgow Museums, Burrell Collection 31.12

11. Sampler made by Frances Cheyney, England, 1663
Silk threads on linen
60.9 cm x 18.4 cm (24 in. x 7 1/4 in.)
Glasgow Museums, Burrell Collection 31.20

12. White work sampler made by Frances Cheyney, England, 1664
Linen and silk threads on linen
64.7 cm x 20.3 cm (25 1/2 in. x 8 in.)
Glasgow Museums, Burrell Collection 31.22

13. Sampler made by Elizabeth Fares, England, 1664
Silk threads on linen
52 cm x 22.8 cm (20 1/2 in. x 9 in.)
Glasgow Museums, Burrell Collection 31.23

14. Sampler made by Jane Turner, England, 1668
Silk and silver threads on linen
66 cm x 16.5 cm (26 in. x 6 1/2 in.)
Glasgow Museums, Burrell Collection 31.8

Detail: Needlework panel depicting Abraham casting out Hagar and Ishmael, mid-17th century, Glasgow Museums, Burrell Collection 29.45

15. Sampler made by CP and Elizabeth Priest, England, 1674 and 1676
Silk threads on linen

75.5 cm x 24.7 cm (29 3/4 in. x 9 3/4 in.)
Glasgow Museums, Burrell Collection 31.5

**16. Sampler made in England,
c.1650–1700**
Silk threads on linen
58.4 cm x 17.8 cm (23 in. x 7 in.)
Glasgow Museums, Burrell Collection 31.4

**17. Sampler made by C K, possibly
south Germany, 1696**
Wool threads on linen
200.6 cm x 48.9 cm (6 ft 7 in. x 19 1/4 in.)
Glasgow Museums, Burrell Collection 31.25

**18. Sampler made by Jane Ann Terrill,
England, c.1700**
Silk threads on linen
81.9 cm x 20.3 cm (32 1/4 in. x 8 in.)
Glasgow Museums, Burrell Collection 31.24

**19. Sampler made by Katy Wood,
Scotland, 1739**
Silk threads on wool
31.4 cm x 21 cm (12 3/8 in. x 8 1/4 in.)
Bequest of Miss Ephan D C Scott, 1934
Glasgow Museums 1934.26.j

**20. Sampler by Mrs Simpson, probably
Scotland, 1765**
Silk threads on linen
29 cm x 19 cm (11 3/8 in. x 7 1/2 in.)
Glasgow Museums E.1979.2.2

**21. Sampler made by Susanna Orr,
America, 1771**
Wool threads on linen
31.1 cm x 21.5 cm (12 1/4 in. x 8 1/2 in.)
Gift of Miss A Fleming, 1938
Glasgow Museums E.1938.80.x

**22. Sampler made by Jean Kerr,
Glasgow, Scotland, c.1802**
Silk and wool threads on wool
45.7 cm x 58.4 cm (18 in. x 23 in.)
Gift of Mr and Mrs A Bailie, 1980
Glasgow Museums E.1980.8

**23. Sampler made by Janet Rankin,
Glasgow, Scotland, 1809**
Wool threads on wool
44.1 cm x 40 cm (17 3/8 in. x 13 3/8 in.)
Gift of Miss A Fleming, 1938
Glasgow Museums E.1938.10.so

**24. Sampler made in Great Britain,
c.1798–1829**
Silk threads on silk
42.5 cm x 66 cm (16 1/2 in. x 26 in.)
Gift of Miss Fraser, 1921
Glasgow Museums 1921.20

**25. Sampler made by PR, Perth,
Scotland, 1809**
Silk threads on wool
47 cm x 34.2 cm (18 1/2 in. x 13 1/2 in.)
Glasgow Museums 1928.36

**26. Sampler made by Margaret Wyllie,
Glasgow, Scotland, 1820**
Silk threads on wool
50.2 cm x 43.1 cm (19 3/4 in. x 17 in.)
Gift of John Murphy, 1928
Glasgow Museums 1928.77

**27. Sampler made by Margaret
Sheddon, New Lanark School, Scotland,
1812**
Silk threads on wool
43.1 cm x 33.5 cm (17 in. x 13 1/8 in.)
Gift of Mrs C Carmichael, 1980
Glasgow Museums E.1980.158

**28. Sampler made by Bethulia Bonner,
Great Britain, 1815**
Silk threads on wool
42.2 cm x 33.6 cm (16 5/8 in. x 13 1/4 in.)
Gift of Miss Morley, 1962
Glasgow Museums E.1962.18.a

**29. Sampler made by Elizabeth
Donald, Aberdeen, Scotland, 1811**
Silk threads on linen
53.2 cm x 33 cm (21 in. x 13 in.)
Gift of Mr and Mrs James Anderson, 1927
Glasgow Museums 1927.18.a

**30. Sampler made by Katherine
Donald, Aberdeen, Scotland, 1820**
Cotton and wool threads on linen
43.1 cm (17 in.) x 32.4 cm (12 3/4 in.); 54 cm x
35.5 cm (21 1/4 in. x 14 in.)
Gift of Mr and Mrs James Anderson, 1927
Glasgow Museums 1927.18.c

Sampler by Isabella Donald, 1814, Glasgow
Museums 1927.18.b

31. Sampler made by Isabella Donald, Aberdeen, Scotland, 1817
Silk threads on linen
23.6 cm x 21.3 cm (9 1/4 in. x 8 1/4 in.)
Gift of Mr and Mrs James Anderson, 1927
Glasgow Museums 1927.18.e

32. Samplers probably made by Isabella Donald, Aberdeen, Scotland, c.1820
Silk threads on cotton
13.5 cm x 11.8 cm (5 3/4 in. x 4 1/2 in.);
10.2 cm x 10.2 (4 1/4 in. x 4 1/4 in.)
Gift of Mr and Mrs James Anderson, 1927
Glasgow Museums 1927.18.f–g

33. Sampler made by Janet McNiel, Scotland, 1819
Wool threads on linen
44.1 cm x 33.5 cm (17 3/4 in. x 13 1/4 in.)
Gift of Miss Cranston, 1927
Glasgow Museums 1927.86.c

34. Sampler from *A Model of the System of Teaching Needlework in the Elementary Schools of the British and Foreign School Society*, Great Britain, 1821
Silk threads on wool
17.8 cm x 11.8 cm (7 in. x 4 1/2 in.)
Museum purchase, 1905
Glasgow Museums 1905.30.a

35. Sampler made by Martha Pollard, Ackworth School, Yorkshire, England, 1811
Wool threads on linen
46 cm x 54 cm (18 1/8 in. x 21 1/4 in.)
Gift of Ernest Noakes, 1962
Glasgow Museums E.1962.7.a

36. Sampler made at Ackworth School, Yorkshire, England, 1826
Silk threads on linen
36.5 cm x 21 cm (14 3/8 in. x 8 1/4 in.)
Gift of Ernest Noakes, 1962
Glasgow Museums E.1962.7.e

37. Sampler made by Priscilla Dell, Ackworth School, Yorkshire, England, 1826
Cotton threads on cotton
19 cm x 19.5 cm (7 1/2 in. x 7 3/4 in.)
Gift of Ernest Noakes, 1962
Glasgow Museums E.1962.7.c

38. Sampler made by Priscilla Dell, Ackworth School, Yorkshire, England, 1827
Silk threads on wool
34.7 cm x 27 cm (13 3/4 in. x 10 5/8 in.)
Gift of Ernest Noakes, 1962
Glasgow Museums E.1962.7.b

39. Sampler made by Elizabeth V Vidal, Scotland, 1824
Silk threads on wool
32 cm x 32.4 cm (12 5/8 in. x 12 3/4 in.)
Glasgow Museums E.1979.2.8

40. Sampler made by Robina Story, Scotland, c.1820–1840
Silk threads on wool
33 cm x 32.5 cm (13 in. x 12 3/4 in.)
Glasgow Museums E.1979.2.19

41. Sampler made by Jessie Henderson, Edinburgh, Scotland, c.1820–1840
Silk threads on wool
49.5 cm x 31.7 cm (19 5/8 in. x 12 1/2 in.)
Glasgow Museums E.1979.2.17

42. Sampler made by Ann Limbird, Bisham School, Berkshire, England, 1827
Silk threads on wool
41.5 cm x 28 cm (16 3/4 in. x 11 in.)
Gift of Amy Anderson, 1915
Glasgow Museums 1915.85

43. Sampler made by Jane Hall, Scotland, 1827
Silk threads on wool
42.5 cm x 31.7 cm (16 3/4 in. x 12 1/2 in.)
Gift of Mrs Jean Bryce Mackie, 1925
Glasgow Museums 1915.50.b

44. Sampler made by Margaret Stewart, Dunkeld, Scotland, 1830
Wool threads on linen
43.1 cm x 21.8 cm (17 in. x 8 1/2 in.)
Gift of Miss Emma Horton, 1919
Glasgow Museums 1919.26.e

45. Sampler made by Margaret Stewart, Dunkeld, Scotland, 1832
Wool threads on wool
23 cm x 22.8 cm (9 in. x 9 in.)
Gift of Miss Emma Horton, 1919
Glasgow Museums 1919.26.f

46. Sampler made by Margaret Stewart, Dunkeld, Scotland, 1833
Wool threads on wool
48.9 cm x 46.8 cm (19 1/4 in. x 18 3/4 in.)
Gift of Miss Emma Horton, 1919
Glasgow Museums 1919.26.g

47. Sampler made by Janet Milne, Glasgow, Scotland, 1831
Silk threads on wool
50.7 cm x 42 cm (120 in. x 6 1/2 in.)
Gift of Miss Buchanan, 1945
Glasgow Museums E.1945.111.2

48. Sampler made by Margaret Stewart, Alloa, Scotland, 1832
Silk threads on linen
42.2 cm x 32 cm (16 5/8 in. x 12 5/8 in.)
Glasgow Museums E.1942.19

49. Sampler made by Elizabeth Yuile, probably England, 1838
Silk threads on wool
39.6 cm x 33 cm (15 5/8 in. x 13 in.)
Gift of Mrs F B Yuile, 1957
Glasgow Museums E.1957.15

50. Sampler made by Elizabeth Smith, Scotland, 1839
Silk threads on wool
53.7 cm x 51.5 cm (21 1/8 in. x 20 1/4 in.)
Gift of Mrs Smith, 1921
Glasgow Museums 1921.24

51. Sampler made by I McK, Great Britain, c.1837–1840
Silk threads on linen
19 cm x 30 cm (7 1/2 in. x 11 3/4 in.)
Museum purchase, 1977
Glasgow Museums E.1977.140

52. Sampler made by Elizabeth Nicholson, Great Britain, 1842
Wool threads on linen
39 cm x 42.5 cm (15 3/8 in. x 16 3/4 in.)
Gift of Mrs Margaret Pringle, 1958
Glasgow Museums E.1958.21

53. Sampler made in Great Britain, mid-19th century
Wool threads and steel beads on cotton
78 cm x 14.6 cm (30 3/4 in. x 5 3/4 in.)
Glasgow Museums E.1942.70.d

54. Miniature shirt made by Catherine Bayne, Gray Abbey School, County Down, Ireland, c.1850–1853
Cotton
23 cm x 41.5 cm (9 1/4 in. x 16 1/4 in.)
Gift of Colonel George MacGregor, 1976
Glasgow Museums E.1976.85

55. Sampler made by Jessie Goldie, Drybridge School, 1864
Wool threads on linen
51.7 cm x 43.1 cm (120 3/8 in. x 7 in.)
Glasgow Museums E.1952.108.d

56. Miniature bodice and skirt, made in Glasgow, Scotland, 1900
Wool with cotton lining
76.1 cm x 47 cm (30 in. x 18 1/2 in.)
Glasgow Museums E.1982.25.1

57. Sampler by Mary Thomson, Glasgow, 1903
Cotton threads on cotton mounted onto card
55.8 cm x 38.1 cm (22 in. x 15 in.)
Gift of Mary E MacKenzie, 2003
Glasgow Museums E.2003.5

Glossary

Band sampler	A sampler with a long and narrow shape.
Black work	Embroidery worked entirely with black thread, often on a white ground. Also known as Spanish work.
Bullion knot	A long knot stitch worked by twisting the thread around the needle before returning it through the fabric.
Chain stitch	A linked, loop stitch that when repeated forms a chain.
Cross stitch	A double stitch in the shape of a diagonal cross. Also known as gros point.
Cut work	Needlework with parts of the fabric cut away to form a pattern, and either in-filled with needle lace or edges embroidered around.
Detached buttonhole stitch	A loop stitch detached from the fabric using the row above as its ground.
Diaper	A small diamond pattern.
Double-running stitch	A variation of running stitch that has a second row of running stitch infilling the gaps. Also known as Holbein and Romanian stitch.
Drawn thread work	Needlework where threads within the weave of the fabric are pulled aside or removed to form a pattern.
Eyelet stitch	A stitch that pulls threads within the weave of the fabric out to form a small hole, or eyelet, in the centre. Also called Algerian eye or bird's eye stitch.
Florentine stitch/ Florentine work	A straight stitch worked in a zigzag design. Also known as Bargello or flame stitch.
Long and short stitch	A variation on satin stitch with the first row of alternating long and short stitches and the infill rows of equal sized stitches.

Long-armed cross stitch	A simple variation of cross stitch with the second diagonal stitch double length and overlapping the next stitch.
Montenegrin stitch	A complex variation of cross stitch with the longer stitches overlapping the next stitch.
Needlepoint fillings / Needle lace	A lace made using a continuous thread and needle, generally worked on parchment, rather than made with many threads on bobbins worked on a pillow.
Picot loop	A loop stitch used in knotted lace or tatting, worked with a shuttle.
Plain weave	A fabric with each warp (vertical) and weft (horizontal) thread woven over one thread and under one thread each time. Also known as tabby weave.
Raised and padded work	Needlework with a raised and padded appearance. Also known during the nineteenth century as stumpwork.
Rococo stitch	A stitch with a series of long stitches held in place with small tacking stitches. Also known as Queen stitch.
Running stitch	The simplest stitch, with evenly spaced regular stitches in a line.
Satin stitch	A straight, parallel stitch sewn close together to fill an area.
Selvage	The side edges of a piece of fabric, often reinforced with stronger threads, sometimes coloured.
Spot motif sampler	A sampler with individual motifs scattered randomly across the fabric.
Stem stitch	A stitch with very slight diagonal overlap.
Tent stitch	A small diagonal stitch worked in horizontal or vertical rows.
Trellis stitch	A stitch worked with a top row of pairs of stitches, with subsequent rows with pairs of stitches sewn at right angles to the row above to form a trellis or lattice design.
White work	Needlework worked entirely with white thread on a white ground.

Further reading

Arthur, Liz, *Embroidery 1600–1700 at the Burrell Collection*, London, John Murray, 1995.

Brooke, Xanthe, *The Lady Lever Art Gallery Catalogue of Embroideries*, Merseyside, National Museums and Galleries on Merseyside, 1992.

Browne, Claire and Wearden, Jennifer, *Samplers from the Victoria & Albert Museum*, London, V&A Publications, 1999.

Clabburn, Pamela, *The Needleworker's Dictionary*, London, Macmillan, 1976.

Clabburn, Pamela, *Samplers*, Buckinghamshire, Shire Publications, 1977.

Colby, Averil, *Samplers*, London, BT Batsford, 1987.

King, Donald and Levey, Santina, *Victoria and Albert Museum's Textile Collection: Embroidery in Britain 1200–1750*, London, V&A Publications, 1993.

Parker, Roziska, *The Subversive Stitch*, London, The Women's Press, 1986.

Shebba, Anne, *Samplers: Five Centuries of a Gentle Craft*, London, Thames & Hudson, 1979.

Swain, Margaret, *Scottish Embroidery*, London, BT Batsford, 1986.

Synge, Lanto, *Antique Embroidery*, London, Blandford Press, 1982.

Synge, Lanto (Ed.), *The Royal School of Needlework Book of Needlework and Embroidery*, London, Collins, 1986.

Synge, Lanto, *Art of Embroidery: History of Style and Technique*, Woodbridge, Suffolk, Antique Collectors' Club, 2001.

Tarrant, Naomi, *Textile Treasures: An Introduction to European Decorative Textiles for Home and Church in the NMS*, Edinburgh, National Museums of Scotland Publishing, 2001.

Witney Antiques, *Diligence, Industry and Virtue: British Samplers and Historic Embroideries*, Witney, Oxfordshire, Witney Antiques, 2002.

Witney Antiques, *An Exceptional Endeavour: British Samplers and Historic Embroideries*, Witney, Oxfordshire, Witney Antiques, 2003.

Places to visit

United Kingdom

Glasgow Museums, The Burrell Collection, Pollok Country Park, Glasgow

Embroiderers' Guild, Hampton Court Palace, Surrey

Fitzwilliam Museum, Cambridge

Lady Lever Art Gallery, Port Sunlight, Liverpool

National Museums of Scotland, Edinburgh

Victoria & Albert Museum, London

Witney Antiques, Oxfordshire

Whitworth Art Gallery, Manchester

United States of America

Cooper-Hewitt, National Design Museum, The Smithsonian Institution, New York

de Young Museum, San Francisco

Los Angeles County Museum of Art, Los Angeles

The Metropolitan Museum of Art, New York

Museum of Fine Arts, Boston

Please remember that displays are subject to change, and it is worth checking before travelling that the items you wish to see are on display.

The Camphill Fund

The Camphill Fund was established in 1984 to promote Glasgow Museums' costume and textiles collection. The Fund takes its name from Camphill House, an eighteenth-century house on the south side of Glasgow, where the collection was formerly housed.

Over the years funds have been raised by holding events such as fashion shows and masked balls, and from generous donations from the business sector. Money from the Fund has gone towards the conservation of the late sixteenth-/early seventeenth-century hangings from Lochleven Castle, the provision of mannequins, exhibitions, and publications on the collection.

Today the collection is housed in the Burrell Collection, Pollok Country Park, Glasgow, where it is available for study and research. The Fund is administered by the Friends of Glasgow Museums (FoGM). If you would like further information on the Fund, or to make a donation, please contact them at the address below.

The Camphill Fund
FoGM
McLellan Galleries
270 Sauchiehall Street
Glasgow G2 3EN
Scotland

camphill fund

PROMOTING
COSTUME &
TEXTILES IN
GLASGOW
MUSEUMS